Raah

Poetic converse through a soul's journey

DNYANADA GHANEKAR

BookLeaf Publishing

Raah

Poetic converse through a soul's journey

© 2024 Dr. Dnyanada Ghanekar

Presentation by *BookLeaf Publishing*

Web: www.bookleafpub.com

E-mail: info@bookleafpub.com

ISBN: 9789358315554

First edition 2024

I thank & love you Aai-Babuji

Dedication

Gratitude

To the Universe for manifesting my

Raah

With love & many thanks to

Ravi, my husband, Rahil, my son,

My in-laws, Baba-Aai,

Mrinal, my sister;

To my Guru, Dr. Rajan Sankaran,

To my healer, Dr. Urvi Chauhan.

To my dear friends,

Dr. Charuvahan V, Yogita Damushte,

Dr. Vaishali Holmukhe,

Dr. Hemangi Nawale, Ketaki Badade,

Sandhya Nerpagar & Mallar Chatterjee,

for always being there.

"How could you reach the pearl by only looking at the sea? If you seek the pearl, be a diver." – Rumi

Foreword

Dnyanada has written verses that resonate with her experiences through various phases of her life. These poems reflect her deep quest for a meaningful existence and touch upon the subtle nature of things. The poems reveal a gentle vulnerability as well as a steadfastness to grasp the intricacies of existence itself through the mirror of observation and experience. Many poems question certain defined truths, to seek what the real truth is.

In this questioning, lies a mind open to learning and growth, just as she has also been in her homeopathic practice and learning. An ardent student of Gurukul, Dnyanada is certainly special and multi-talented.

This 'Raah' is just the beginning of her foray into self-expression through the medium of poetry. I heartily congratulate her as well as wish her well for all her future projects.

Rajan Sankaran
2023

Firsts are always precious, be that falling (or probably rising) in love or any meaningful endeavor. The fragrance of firsts sparkles up one's spirit bringing in the necessary fuel to room and bloom. "Raah" is Dnyanada's first too, her love as well as her endeavor merging in oneness here.

I have known more of Dnyanada as her therapist and have witnessed a fiery spirit that her being beholds. It brings me pleasure to witness her inner fire channeling itself into a valuable expression.

When it comes to poetry, each honest one that originates from rich personal experience arrives with a unique fragrance, bringing in the experience of a *precious first* to its poet as well as to its audience! That's the hidden beauty of poetry and its unique gift to all.

With "Raah", Dnyanada is taking her first courageous step to pass on these fragrances to the world.

Fragrance when inhaled slowly and received warmly, spread out its magic gently. I enjoyed the unique aromas present in "Raah" of all, Breath, Childhood, Sometimes, Nothing matters – managed to touch my heart the most - not just the words but their deeper message. Presented poems are expressions of her experiences earned navigating through the road (Raah) of her life and any honest expressions are always potent and promising in their offering. I am certain these poems will manage to find their righteous place and meet the righteous objectives for which they are being offered here.

I wish Dnyanada the very best with her first fragrant endeavor as well as all the following ones.

For, any beginning secretly holds fertile seeds in its womb!

Dr Urvi Chauhan
12th Nov. 2023
Afternoon

Table of contents

Childhood
Tree
Birds
Death
Rest
Wait
Calling

Preface

Life is a process with its sweet ups and downs. It is how we perceive and take each stride, to either sink in or to make an ascent is our choice. It took me a long time to realize this until a storm shook me. In the process, to hurt and to get hurt was inevitable. Ultimately, I was left with only two choices: losing my close ones or rising above my limitations. To rise above the, 'I', to accept, to free myself and that of the other, to connect to the higher realm, where nothing remains.

And I chose the latter, it's a journey in continuum. Every time, when I experienced intense emotions of grief, anger, fear, panic, happiness, loneliness, etc. words just dropped and got transformed into poetic clusters, manifesting my *raah*.

In this journey, I dive deeper into myself, become aware, and enjoy the aroma and the taste of each flavor that lies in the vastness of life and its experience.

People we happen to meet in our lives whether by chance or not, pleasant or unpleasant are nothing but mirrors that reflect ourselves.

Raah, is an extension of myself, a piece of my heart and art.

The peepal leaf that travels with each poem's title takes me to the joyous moments of my childhood spent under the tree's shade, making me feel blessed and grateful.

Be it a coiling up of a snail or a free-flying butterfly, each one's journey is unique and beautiful. It has no answer, reason, or logic as to why and how. It is just as it is.

Soul

Then again, I found someone very good

at heart,

And I ran to pour out my inner hurt

part.

Just to find someone who again

shattered me apart,

And it took so many years to collect

those pieces fallen apart.

Now that I am too tired to either feel

good or to feel sad,

I just close off and sit for a while,

Filled with emotions wild.

Deep down my soul said,

"I am your unwavering reality,

So why these shackles?

And you sought love from outside

always.

Oh, you beautiful soul, the divine rests

in you.

Why have you come all the way to find

me in you?

You are a treasure box of endless joy,

The magic lies within you."

A smile just tickled my cheek,

And it whispered to me,

What you seek is there within you.

Further, the soul said, "Hug me and I

shall be eternal in thee, you shall be in

peace with yourself forever."

The moment just transpired,

Making its ripples on me,

And the very moment became immortal

in me.

Let me be here for a while.

Time

It's as if life runs on your tickle,

And you keep tickling,

Even now my ears can hear.

So, tell me,

Do both of you intersect at any point?

What an irony, that time has been asked

for its own time!

Do you not get tired of being in motion

all the time?

And whom do you share your worries

with?

Do you remember your past, present,

And how your future might be?

People said we had our bad times,

People also said we had our good times.

But time is undefined, and so is life.

Time for life and life for time,

Both go hand in hand.

Neither do they intersect, nor do they

compete.

Love be this way, in unbounded sway,

Making their journey, their way.

Breath

One fine morning,

A thought crossed my mind,

About what life is!

I closed my eyes pondering over a bit,

And while I inhaled and exhaled deep,

To my utter surprise,

Life just ended in that one breath.

I couldn't describe life,

But I experienced life at that very

moment.

As I opened my eyes, I saw a beautiful

blooming flower, Fuschia in color.

I was mesmerized,

It was overflowing with fragrance,

Without itself having any.

Mask

And now a very thin line remains,

For the soul and the mask to separate.

The mask is now dying to unveil itself,

So desperate and in utter disgrace.

Pushing the soul and rising high,

But the fool has forgotten that the

essence lies in its very own soul.

The mask, not knowing that it is lost,

Rises still higher to the burning flame of

its glory!

The cheers are high,

The applauses seem huge,

Losing all its vanity,

The mask thus separates from its soul.

With both entities now apart,

The mask, higher into the sky,

And the poor soul deep down in the

abyss.

The mask looks down onto the ground

with contempt,

thereby deepening its wound.

The mask shines,

But all that glitters is not gold, a saying

very old.

The mask is unaware that it has to fade

sooner or later.

But the soul, its essence is eternal.

Slowly the applauses begin to fade,

With the fiery flames turning icy cold.

The mask is nowhere, in its

desperation to be everywhere,

Searching for its identity in the lost

flames.

Finally, it comes to know that all that is

left is just snow,

It craves warmth now.

It needs to be sane, to wave off the

insane, being tired of the rat race.

In the ashes fallen,

All in vain.

It calls out loud for its beloved one,

its very own soul.

"I swayed away in fullness,

And now left only with emptiness.

Now I remember you, my dear soul,

You were with me forever.

Unaffected by pleasure and pain,

Without you, I am nothing,

But a thing incomplete."

Said the mask to the soul, and they were

together forever.

Strings of attachment

I saw a dreamcatcher with colorful

feathers woven into it,

I kept watching it,

I paused, and a thought came.

The feathers are yearning to fly,

to be free,

For what they are meant to be.

The feather has to live its dream now.

So with no strings attached to itself,

It takes a huge leap and flies high,

It feels light, and it feels free.

When it looks back to the dreamcatcher,

The place it was once tethered,

It bows down in gratitude.

It was only then, that it became aware,

Of its true freedom,

Of not being woven,

Into something,

But in setting itself free.

The feather is awestruck,

That it has traveled so far.

It has now to seek, beyond the

boundaries of

Freedom and restriction,

Of light and dark,

To the space itself.

Will it be able to just be?

And the feather keeps watching

the blank space.

Lonely

Lonely space with lone me,

The day seems long,

With the twilight along,

And the night just passes by.

I look up at the sky,

It seems so vacant.

With the orange crescent alone,

And yet so filled with the twinkling

stars.

Every breath is alone,

Not waiting nor staying,

But it reminds me of the ongoing life

each time.

Is this endless loneliness in this,

Not immortal life, a permanence?

Or is this me who feels lonely inside

endlessly?

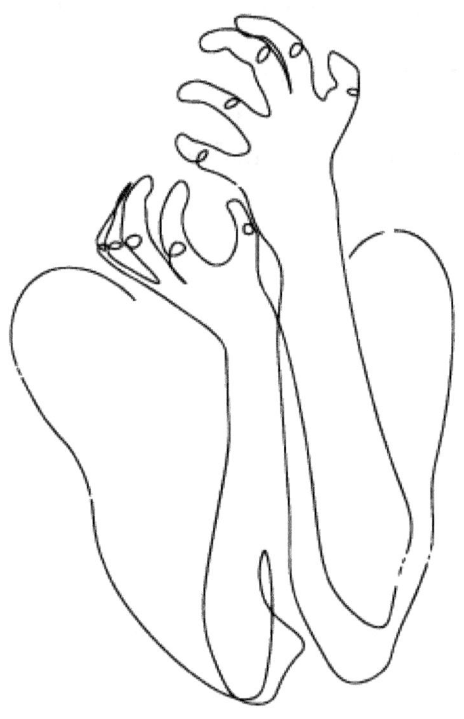

Pain

I have been through pain,

agonizing and intense,

The harder I tried to get away,

The more it engulfed me.

Sometimes it choked my throat,

Sometimes I felt the ground sinking in.

The more I held on,

The more it slipped away from my hand.

It made me frantic,

I was shouting insanely,

But my voice was unheard.

There was no one, except a miserable

me.

I was silent, the silence I had forgotten

living through this pain.

Until I heard the gush of air,

That knocked my chest and it kept

knocking,

Till the time I became aware of my

breath.

At that moment I felt like a lost ship

had found its shore,

I felt like I belonged.

I felt as if a lost child had found its

mother.

A feeling so relieving.

It was a thrust of trust that my breath

gave me,

And I just kept flowing with it.

I felt as if love was flowing within me,

Love caressed my pain,

I could feel its touch,

As if droplets of love kissed my pain,

and dissolved in me.

Torn

So what if you are torn apart?

Try to gather yourself slowly.

So what if it takes time?

Time alone shall heal.

So what if you are broken?

Stand in grace.

So what if it takes time?

Time alone shall heal.

So what if the wings have lost their

ability to fly?

Let them gather with all their might,

Their lost glory,

Time alone shall heal.

Just allow yourself to unfold slowly,

Letting that inner fear find its vent,

Through your wings spread wide apart,

And the trust emanating from each

breath.

Through the hundred times broken you,

And though looking broken,

This piece of you

Shall rediscover the once-hidden

beautiful self,

That no one shall ever,

Ever be able to part from you.

Scars

Scars are gorgeous,

They talk about things magnanimous.

Of the armor you put to fit,

And of the times when you got hit.

Rumi once said, "Wound is the place

where the light enters you."

A scar is ugly,

But a beauty hidden deep, rather than a

Beauty that's just a

facade.

Rose

Sometimes I just live,

And die in a moment or two.

Sometimes life seems so expansive,

That I just want to live it fully.

Sometimes it seems like a burden,

That I want to unburden.

At last, the mortal rose,

Has also to shed its pride.

Being vulnerable though, how subtly,

It sings the song of its falling,

gracefully.

Nothing matters

It dawned on me late,

But it's never too late.

No matter if you are nowhere,

No matter if no one appreciates you,

Or if you are mocked,

Believe in yourself

When no one does.

Trust yourself,

When no one does.

Embrace yourself,

Love, and accept the way you are

When no one does.

You are unique and beautiful,

No matter if no one tells you,

Or you never hear,

from anyone, anytime.

Beauty

Beauty is ethereal,

Beauty is a creation that just happens.

None, ever able to trace its creator.

Beauty is mysterious,

Untouched, and pure,

Only the charms of nature,

aware may be.

Beauty is undefinable,

A thing just to be.

Beauty neither lies in the living nor

the dead.

Blessed are the souls,

Who can perceive the dead leaf fallen

onto the ground,

Surrendering its beauty to the unbound.

Dark Love

She is hidden, but her smile lightens up

everything,

She fears but loves beyond.

She had many questions,

And she found the answers in him.

He is hidden, but he's out there, come

what may,

He embraces his fears, his love is the

universe.

He has no questions, but he is a question

in himself.

When she meets him,

It's a pure blossoming, no intentions, no

targets,

Just the feeling without an inch of

touch.

They just soak in each other's eyes

without a blink,

To watch the depth, but it's unending.

They love, they heal, and they spread

their light in silence.

Can such a beautiful thing be possible?

Someone said it's love.

You

Gentle breeze,

I am thinking of you.

Drizzling rain,

I am thinking of you.

Blooming flowers,

I am thinking of you.

Falling leaves,

I am thinking of you.

Rising Sun,

I am thinking of you.

Floating clouds,

I am thinking of you.

Tickling clock,

I am thinking of you.

I walk alone,

Thinking of you.

I watch,

The Glowing Moon,

Thinking of You.

I talk to someone,

Thinking of you.

I write something,

Thinking of you.

I'll be waiting somewhere,

Thinking of you.

I know not anytime,

Thinking of you.

I know now at the same time,

You are thinking of me!

Fallen

I have fallen,

How?

I don't know.

I have fallen,

Where?

Somewhere I don't know!

I have fallen,

When?

Time I didn't know!

I have fallen,

In the ocean?

No, it's deeper still.

I have fallen,

Get up then.

No, I can't.

I have fallen,

Painful?

No, it is much more.

I have fallen,

and I keep falling,

Again and again,

In love,

Into you,

In You.

Hidden

How I fear my fear,

Of the untied ties, that they will break.

Of the unsaid words, that will get heard,

Of the untainted, that will get stained.

Of the space, that will be invaded,

Of the self, that will be no more.

Of the teardrop, that will just fall,

And unveil the pain beneath.

Fear

Fear has gripped me,

Caught me in it,

The web is quite intricate,

Though it seems very delicate,

I am in deep unrest,

Suffocating myself with not a single

moment of rest.

I don't know when and how this shall

end.

Fear has gripped me,

Spreading far and wide,

I can see nothing except that high tide.

I don't know when and how I'll be able

to free myself.

Fear has gripped me,

Nothing remains but sheer panic,

Weaving a web around me,

Embedding the darkness in it.

I don't know when and how this shall

end.

Fear has gripped me,

the dark shadows hovering in the sky,

Covering, making it more and more

beclouded,

Hope seems to have closed its doors,

Neither the light can knock anymore.

I don't know when and how I'll be able

to free myself.

Fear has gripped me,

Leaving me in misery,

Wrenched and drenched in it,

Time and moments both have passed,

untouched.

I don't know when and how this shall

end.

Now the only way out,

Is the way in,

Choices are very few, with no one to my

rescue.

But I shall come out of this web,

Is a promise not futile,

And no more be its slave.

I will win over, time is not the same,

Every second's a different game.

Heart

It's a story of a heart, not much time has

passed

When the heart used to sway back and

forth,

Hither and thither.

Validation was all it needed and

the only way it existed, it thought!

So, it stumbled upon many hearts,

good at heart.

Alas! Which didn't ever fulfill it.

Until a day came when the heart felt

almost heart-broken,

Tired of the story it had been living,

For so many years.

And it's only when one is shaken,

That one tries to wake up,

And focus on oneself.

The outside hardly matters then,

It happened the same with the

heart,

Tears just poured,

Cleansing the heart's soul.

The joy it experienced was profound,

There was no one except the heart,

No one to validate,

No place to reach,

But just being with itself,

And being itself,

Felt grateful.

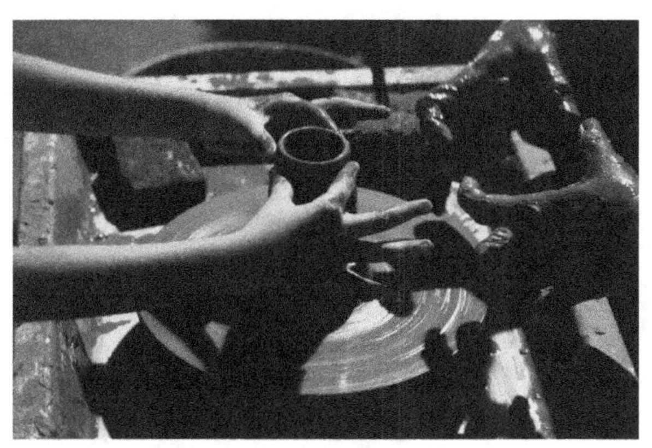

Hold & let go

But it's only the 'I' that questions,

For which it has no answers,

But, how do I let go,

Of what I am holding onto?

My life in a nutshell

was to hold on and

let go,

It was not easy though.

The more I hold onto it, the more I get

away,

And the more I let go,

the more I come closer.

What you hear, I hear the same.

What you feel, I feel the same,

Then why am I still holding on,

and to whom?

To hold is to stagnate.

To flow is to connect to your higher self,

Breaking your limits,

The journey is to transcend,

To watch the beautiful metamorphosis

happening,

Turning a larva into a butterfly,

And then losing one's self,

Being one with the consciousness,

Will this ever happen?

Let me embark on the next page of my

journey.

Undefined

Some things can't be defined,

They just can't be.

They are beyond any definition,

Boundaries, limits, and words.

Yes, but they can be felt,

sensed deeply,

Where only silence resides.

Truth is simple.

There is, no if, but, how; it is just there.

It uplifts the burden of everything.

No sounds, no words, no questions

anymore,

No answers thereby.

Nothing remains, nothing goes.

But yes, there is a thing that remains

That remains the way it is.

Past

Past was crumpled yet beautiful,

Which I knew not then,

Which I know now.

Messy at times,

But it journeyed me through it,

To a complete meaningful existence.

Searching for meaning isn't a norm

always,

But seeking one's self is.

Which I knew not then,

Which I know now.

Sometimes I crave so much for it,

That I want to get hold of it anyhow,

And sometimes I run so wild,

That I want to escape it somehow.

In the end,

I stand neutral,

For I can't get either of them,

For this moment is also passing by,

Becoming a past,

And what remains is only the now.

Tears

I have seen tears,

tears in the eyes very tired,

Tears of someone,

Long estranged from self.

Tears of someone who

Incessantly kept running from

himself,

So scared to meet his lonely self.

His tears hid beneath the keys of his

piano,

While he played it.

His tears hid in his smile,

And the tears just froze once.

Until a day came,

When love flashed just once,

And the tears began to melt.

Being overtly

sensitive,

They just dropped themselves on his

care-woven face.

His face lit up like never before,

It was beautiful to watch the tears

flowing,

It felt so relieving, so forgiving,

It gave a vent to the deeper suffering

inside,

Of years together.

There was total silence,

There was a yearning for love,

There was closeness,

There was warmth exuding,

there was just us,

The smiles lit our eyes, there was love.

Ripples

Unaware, of when the ripples in the sea,

Of my thoughts become huge,

And the chaos hits me like waves.

Sometimes I get submerged,

Sometimes they just tickle my feet and

emerge.

They try to take hold of me many a time,

And then the rudder for my rescue,

Comes to pull me through,

sometimes.

The journey of the waves and the ripples

Will go on and on,

With the rudder or without it;

But the huge sea shall remain.

Wanderer

Wandering through the lanes of a place

called the land of religious sanctuary,

Dharamshala,

I came across this man,

In not a very crowded place.

He was with his guitar.

He was nowhere but with himself.

And so was the tune so wonderful in

itself.

Around him were some old rags.

His expression was so intense,

His devotion to music in that moment,

He just merged with his inner self.

Little did he care for who was around,

Being mesmerized by his deep inner

sound.

People came and people left,

Some dropped a few coins.

But this soul was just immersed,

In his musical charm.

After playing his heart out on the guitar,

He got up in silence and gathered his

stuff.

He had lived his moment to the fullest,

By playing his tune to its utmost.

Purple

As I walked by,

I saw a fragile,

transparent purple flower,

With its imprint on the ground.

I kept watching until a question nudged

me,

Can there be love,

Without being in love?

The relationship itself binds,

Can there be a relationship without

being in a relationship?

And the question remains....

Sometimes

Sometimes, I wonder,

How the trees are

rooted in the dark,

And the leaves so

cheerful in the sunlight,

Swaying in every direction of the wind

that passes by.

Sometimes I wonder,

How the earth has all our footprints,

Without having any of its own.

Sometimes I wonder,

How the sun shines,

bright and gay every day,

Despite the last day's worry.

And how the flowers bloom, so colorful,

Pouring their sweet smell all around.

Sometimes I wonder how the

leaves fall so rhythmic.

Sometimes I wonder,

How the mind raises such complexities,

And how the beauty of nature lies in its

simplicity!

Childhood

Gone are the days running under the

sun's rays,

Careless, naive, and free,

Wandering and humming like a bee.

As I sit sipping my tea, looking down

from my window pane,

It takes me to my childhood lane.

The hustle and bustle,

hearing the dry leaves rustle,

Where the little things seemed so big,

And the narrow lanes so wide,

Where small distances seemed so long.

Gone are the days when a single coin,

Would bring a broad smile,

And dissolve our grin.

The colorful soap bubbles, the candies,

And those suckles.

The toffee, the fun, and the play,

At which our life would just sway.

The crying faces on day one of our

school,

And the smiling faces having those ices

cool.

Hopping in the drenching rain,

Where everything else was in vain.

Where everyone thought they were

smart,

Well, that was one of life's art.

Listening to my Grandma's stories,

And feeling the touch of her robust

hands,

Which I still yearn for.

Gone are those golden days.

As I flip through my diary pages,

It has been ages,

But the childhood memory feels like a

raindrop,

Freshly fallen onto the ground,

And this earthy smell takes me,

Through the doors of my childhood.

Tree

I saw what I didn't,

I was but I was not,

Maybe I became the everything in me.

Be one like a tree,

With its branches reaching the sky high.

But its roots,

Deep under the Earth.

At times, with a hollow in its trunk,

It still flourishes,

Nurturing other lives,

Under its soothing shade,

The beings feel heavenly.

It says it has no story of its own,

But it has lived through numerous

stories,

It says, being you is enough.

It's said, giving is divine,

An unconditional love.

It gloriously takes a stance,

And keeps dancing to the

universal song unknown.

Birds

I want to be one like you,

Take me with you, teach me how to fly.

I have feathers,

But my mind tithers, and my soul

flitters.

I want to be one like you,

Tell me how the sky feels,

Is it the same way as the earth to my

heels?

I want to be one like you,

Where words don't matter,

Of all the worldly chatter.

I want to be one like you,

Grounded at one end,

Soaring in the sky at the other end,

Yet humble towards the end.

I want to be one like you.

Oh, you wonderful bird,

Spiritual and aware,

So common yet so rare.

Death

I suddenly felt an upsurge of emotions,

And how we are full of notions.

What a moment it was,

I was unaware,

Till the time a teardrop made its way

through my

eyes to my heart.

Touched me very deeply,

My heart, too full to hold it,

I just let it go.

At that very moment,

I learned a bit about life,

Life seemed shorter now,

Death could knock at any moment.

No time for matters petty.

The start of a new journey

from

meaningless to meaningful.

Love was gushing out,

May the starving souls fill their vacuum.

May the dead ones find peace,

May the living souls be a contagion,

Spirits full of compassion.

Rest

I have met someone,

Who has traveled a long way,

And whose eyes speak of the numerous

struggles.

Oh, dear traveler, you have come so far,

You need rest, you need peace.

Under the soothing canopy,

calming refuge and relaxing shelter

of this magnificent

Banyan tree, surrender yourself.

The self that fought so many wars,

The war of love, of separation,

The bitterness, the numerous sorrows,

And the suffering, you thought

unending, all shall ease.

Oh, dear traveler, you have come so far,

You need rest, you need peace.

Drop this self and you shall be free.

Under the haven of this sky,

Being in Mother Earth's lap,

We are united now,

We are the same, the inherent nature,

Don't you bind yourself in you,

We both being just nothing,

but a part of everything.

Oh, dear traveler, you have come so far,

You need rest, you need peace.

Wait

I waited and waited,

It was so long that I forgot, I wanted it.

And then it just came out of nowhere,

When the longing was no more.

And then I am taken all along with it,

I am flowing, I am laughing, I am crying,

I want to cling to it.

But I am afraid, what if it's a dream?

And it vanishes once I am awake!

But I am in the moment,

Which is now, without

the burden of knowing

time, space,

And being,

And knowing myself.

Calling

My calling is different from yours,

The ultimate reach is the same,

But the ways aren't.

But don't you worry wanderer,

We will connect at some point.

Let me know how your journey was,

And so will I, of mine.

Let us breathe for a while,

And be prepared for our next mile.

It's not about the

destination,

Because the journey in itself is a

sublimation,

A soulful alienation.

To write is to love

To love is to write

Love begins at home

A home is a place where you belong

To belong is to love

Everyone wants to travel back home.

Raah dhundte dhundte na jane kab usi raah par chal diye.

Your thoughts, suggestions, and
comments are highly welcome.
Do write to me about how you feel about
- Raah
Email id- dnyana434@gmail.com
Insta id- dnyanadaghanekar
Facebook id-Dnyanada Ghanekar